Acts of generosity

The ability of generosity to transform a person's heart, life, and the world

Raymond H.boyd

Table of contents

Chapter 1

What is the demonstration of giving?

Generosity is more than a way of
behaving. Being
Generosity is described as uninhibitedly
giving beneficial things. It is frequently
uninhibited, unhindered, and liberal.
The fact that a great deal like
unselfishness makes generosity a
quality. Somebody showing generosity is
glad to give time, cash, food, or
consideration to individuals out of luck.

Generosity is a quality — like
genuineness and persistence — that we
as a whole presumably wish we had a
greater amount of. At the point when you
show generosity, you could offer things or
cash or put others before yourself. Be

that as it may, generosity is about more than money and stuff. While you're excusing and delicate to individuals, you show generosity of soul. Assuming you give others help or credit, that shows generosity. The world would unquestionably be a superior spot if more individuals showed generosity to other people

In the same way as other small children, you might bear in mind in primary school finding out about the ethics we ought to live by; the rundown of characteristics that are considered 'ethically great'. In the rundown, you might have found characteristics like perseverance, persistence, consideration, lowliness, and generosity. This season, we frequently hear some extra about generosity. Generosity is the demonstration of giving broadly and abundantly. Since December is the 'time of giving' there could be no greater chance to take a gander at straightforward ways of being liberal this season.

So presently you might be asking, for what reason is generosity significant throughout everyday life? Indeed, many individuals have investigated the advantages of generosity. What's more, the extraordinary news is, there are so many! Individuals who are more liberal are in many cases more joyful, more satisfied, and happy with their lives. Something stands out about how rewarding others helps you have an improved outlook on yourself consequently. In addition to the fact that it causes individuals to feel more certain, however, you are many times much more useful when they are liberal.

Albeit the Christmas season is known for generosity, it is essential all year! One more astonishing advantage of liberal giving is the positive effect you can have on others' lives. Not exclusively will you receive rewards for your giving, however you never know the impact you can have on another person? Whether you are carrying a warm feast to another mother, giving cash to your nearby fire station, or investing energy at the nursing home down the road, these liberal demonstrations can go far.

Notice there isn't anything explicit in that frame of mind about giving cash, even though it can incorporate cash. This is significant because the majority of us liken generosity to giving cash. The risk with just seeing this as a monetary exchange is that you could miss the genuine inspiration driving giving, which is graciousness, and benevolence. Just when these inspirations are available are the advantages of giving understanding.

Generosity is dramatic
Being caring, sacrificial, and providing for others ends up being great for us. At the point when we provide for somebody, it reacts to, meaning our giving spikes them and others likewise to give. It's outstanding! Thoughtful gestures and generosity have an increasing impact, and there's a mental justification for this. What impact could it have on your life and your business if you somehow happened to expand your degree of generosity? What regions might you at any point utilize your abilities and gifts to a greater extent and with more effect? What we see is that individuals who increment their generosity ordinarily see

the profit from that generosity return increased, for example, you need to provide for getting. Furthermore, when you give huge of your time and abilities you get that energy back into your business, profession, or individual life.

What might occur on the planet if we as a whole were dedicated to expanding the time we spent being liberal by 1 hour seven days? That would be another hour to tutor somebody who is contemplating changing vocations or beginning a business, another hour to spend training an undergrad on the most proficient method to make that progress into the functioning scene effectively, and another hour spent assisting our companions at work with pondering our choices and approaches contrastingly to drive more prominent outcomes in our associations. What effect could that have on our reality and our general surroundings? I challenge you to find another hour or seven days to live liberally and see what sort of effect the generosity impact could have on you!

Generosity is infectious
The piece of our mind related to joy, social association, and trust gets invigorated when we are liberal, causing us to feel all warm and fluffy inside. This happens whether we are the provider or we witness a demonstration of generosity. Recollect the last scene in the film "It's A Magnificent Life?" The bank analyst, Carter, for those of you who can easily forget his name, who nearly shut down the Bailey Building and Credit, winds up giving of his cash to save it all things being equal. Why? Basic, he became involved with the generosity free for all that was going on.

It's infectious, and it's the most profound thing we have the honor of doing.

In a review, members were given cash and afterward haphazardly doled out to one of two gatherings. One gathering was to utilize the cash to spend on themselves while the other gathering was to spend the cash on others. Endlessly time once more, the gathering that spends the cash on others revealed a more prominent degree of satisfaction. These discoveries were demonstrated through fMRI, which affirmed the immediate association between generosity and satisfaction. Giving encourages us.

Chapter 2

Justifications for why an individual ought to be generous

Generous giving is self-advantageous (9:6).
Generous giving is self-intrigued in that it benefits ourselves — we sow generously so we can procure generously.

This sounds like the "flourishing gospel" taught by numerous TV preachers. In any case, the people who utilize this refrain to push such a "gospel" misjudge and abuse this stanza.

Paul only purposes a natural cultivating saying — "more yields come from utilizing more seed." This is a straightforward and verified reality. Maxims 11:24-25 advances this same truth. God will give us all that we want.

The Bible gives no ironclad commitment to actual flourishing. Christ, Himself was poor. These refrains aren't natural keys to monetary abundance. Our longing ought to be for a bigger gathering. We sow generously to, in this manner, harvest generously to God's magnificence. Provide for the Lord's work generously, particularly crafted by the nearby church.

Supplicate that your congregation's longing consistently is to build the level of the financial plan that goes to mission work abroad.

 Generous giving is God-satisfying (9:7) God thinks often about the inspiration for giving. A secularist sees God as consistently satisfied. one. Notwithstanding, the Bible says that God is sacred, and that implies that He is just for that which is great and right. His sacredness is satisfied by merry giving, not giving under commitment.

We aren't under the impulse to give. No place in the New Testament does it order giving as is drilled and told in the Old Testament. Notwithstanding, giving is bigger than the Mosaic Covenant. Abraham and Jacob both exhibit giving before the Mosaic Covenant.

The norm for giving is higher in the New Testament. We are told to give merrily, not out of impulse, but rather because we need to give. To give merrily, we want another heart for change.

Paul maintains that the Corinthians in this entry should comprehend the open door they need to accommodate the

Believers in Jerusalem. Jesus said in Matthew 10:8: "Freely you have gotten, unreservedly give." "happy" in 2 Corinthians 9:7 signifies "entertaining."

What might you at any point provide for God and His work that you're not giving? Keep in mind, that God cherishes a bright provider. Give unreservedly and you will know the wonders of knowing God.

Generous giving is certain (9:8-10) Generous giving is certain that giving is correct and that God will supply every one of your necessities. The one who fears the Lord is generous.

As Christians, we comprehend that our wrongdoings have been excused in Christ. Our lives have been changed, passing on us with the longing and drive to give generously to other people.

Christian, why call yourself a Christian if you don't give? The fact that God will supply makes generous giving certain. It's anything but a commitment to success. You needn't bother with being rich to be generous. All you want is to be content (Philippians 4:11).

Christian, how might your giving for Christ's function contrast with your diversion financial plan?

The incomparable Puritan Richard Baxter requested his giving thusly:

Normal necessities (ex. food and haven);
Public important great (ex. charges);
Youngsters;

Genuine poor (ex. poor inside the
congregation); and,
Common poor;
Comforts.

How might your financial plan compare to
these models?

Generous giving is acclaim inciting
(9:11-13)
Generous giving carries commendation
to God.

"Perform" in refrain 12 is "ritual," and that
implies playing out the help of
accommodating God's kin.

What separates laud from your spirit?
We give generously eventually so God
will be said thanks to and adulated. In
our submission, God is adulated. Our
little submissions of giving will deliver

torrential slides of good. Generous giving likewise incites others to laud God.

Generous giving doesn't need to be monetary. Consider the individual who gives generously of their opportunity to impart the Gospel to one individual, or to welcome an individual to chapel — and the exceptional effect that might have in time.

Be more generous than seems OK, more sympathetic than is required, more confident than the realities direct, more driving forward than anyone merits, all because the gospel is valid
Generous giving is guaranteeing (9:13a)
Generous giving guarantees us and others the truth of pronouncing Christ. Giving generously is the approval crafted by Christ in your life. We realize that salvation is with conviction alone, in

Christ alone, yet we additionally realize that the Bible instructs that our confidence is affirmed in our works (James 2).

For instance, what does the declaration of your checkbook say regarding your confidence?

In the good news of John, we read that Jesus Christ set out his life for us. Following His model we see these Greek Christians setting out their lives for their Jewish siblings. Something could never occur beyond salvation.

Generous giving is collaborating in and for the good news of Jesus Christ (9:13b) Generous giving is participating in and for the Gospel of Jesus Christ. You ought to give for partnership.

The Corinthians gave in light of their adoration for Christ. The Gospel unites common polarities.

The Gospel is clarified by our cooperation. Dedicated giving prompts remarkable partnership.

In your dedicated providing for your congregation, you support preachers all over the planet, Bible interpretation, assisting the vulnerable, and thus significantly more — consequences of which we won't have the foggiest idea about this side of paradise.

. The generous offering is evangelistic because it attracts consideration to the Savior (9:14-15)

Generous giving is evangelistic. The reason for Paul's admonishment is the Gospel of Christ. The unbelievable gift is the gospel, the comprehension that the nobility of God pardons our wrongdoings. How God has helped us in Christ is unbelievable (John 3:16).

What gospel is our giving showing, as a congregation and as people? Does our giving exhibit a "remuneration gospel" or one of an indefinable gift?

We find in Acts 24 that Paul did convey this gift from the Corinthians to the Christians in Jerusalem.

What have we gained from this antiquated demonstration of acquiescence?

Chapter 3

How might somebody be more generous?

Generosity appears to tumble to the wayside once the special seasons are finished. All in all, how might you be more liberal in your routine?

What you can give? The wellspring of your generosity will rely upon your life conditions. A portion of the things you can be liberal with are:

Cash
Time
Help
Assets and items
Support
Basic reassurance
Why you ought to be more liberal.
Generosity can prompt an astonishing

number of advantages when drilled routinely. Normally, helping other people will help them. Be that as it may, being liberal will help you right away and in the long haul.

Stationary individuals who volunteer will quite often turn out to be all the more truly dynamic, working on there in general actual wellbeing.
Liberal individuals will generally live longer.
Generosity makes individuals more joyful, working on there, generally speaking, psychological wellness.
Chipping in and generosity forestall burnout with how much work individuals can do.
Generosity improves and reinforces relational connections.
Might you at any point figure out how to be liberal? Anybody can be liberal.

Studies have shown that people are normally disposed to be liberal. Nonetheless, certain individuals need additional direction to draw out that secret generosity.

Prescribed Ways Of being More Liberal
Be liberal with your appreciation.
A straightforward "bless your heart" can mean everything. Gifts and good cause work are extraordinary ways of offering in return, however offering your certified appreciation for loved ones can support their mindset, as well. Furthermore, appreciation likewise works on your connections — and rehearsing thanks can likewise make you more liberal after some time. It's a shared benefit win![1]
You can thank somebody any time, for anything. Message your mother suddenly: "Was simply contemplating all

that you've accomplished for me. Many thanks."

At the point when you notice that your child made a garbage run, leave him a note in front of him with his #1 confection: "Thank you kindly, honey! You rock."

If your accomplice stands by listening to you vent about an extreme issue, say thanks to them for their sympathetic ear. "I want to believe that you know the amount I value this — I truly expected to talk."

Compliment individuals around you

We as whole respect liberal individuals — so for what reason could it at any point be so hard to turn into a giving individual? With occupied plans and instilled propensities, setting aside a few minutes for generosity might feel like a test. In any case, there are lots of fast (and free!) ways of rewarding your local area and thoroughly having an effect. Beneath, we've arranged a rundown of ways you can offer back right this second. To figure out how you can turn into a more liberal individual, read on!

Be liberal with your appreciation.

A straightforward "much obliged" can mean everything. Gifts and good cause work are incredible ways of offering in return, yet offering your veritable appreciation for loved ones can support their mindset, as well. In addition, appreciation likewise works on your connections — and rehearsing thanks can likewise make you more liberal after some time. It's a mutual benefit win![1] You can thank somebody any time, for anything. Message your mother all of a sudden: "Was simply contemplating all that you've accomplished for me. Thank you kindly."

At the point when you notice that your child made a garbage run, leave him a note in front of him with his number one sweet treat: "Thank you kindly, honey! You rock."

If your accomplice stands by listening to you vent about an extreme issue, say thanks to them for their compassionate ear. "I want to believe that you know the amount I value this — I truly expected to talk."

Compliment individuals around you.

Individuals misjudge the force of genuine commendations. By telling somebody that their hair sparkles or their work rocks, you can change their day, support their mindset, and raise their certainty.

Offer explicit, authentic commendations consistently. Simply make sure to keep them proper; respecting somebody's thorough searches in the working environment, for example, is not a smart thought. [2]

Give a youngster access to your life and know that you're glad for them: "I want to believe that you know how magnificent I think you are. You're so energetic about science — it's astounding."

Let your clerk know that they have an extraordinary look: "I was unable to cherish those nails more. You have a good time, exceptional style!"

Leave a tomfoolery note on your neighbor's entryway: "Your Halloween enhancements look Astounding. I could barely handle it. So great!"

Perform irregular thoughtful gestures.

You needn't bother with a reason or coordinated occasion to bring somebody happiness. Arbitrary thoughtful gestures are about abrupt motivation, honest goals, and getting imaginative. Require one moment to think — what unprompted thing might you at any point do right now to light up somebody's day? Not exclusively will your signal make their week, yet it could likewise rouse them to show preemptive kindness, too.[3]

Make a genuine card for individuals in hospice care. On the off chance that you have children, include them. Not exclusively will you be showing generosity, yet a kid's imagination can make these cards considerably really contacting.

Go through the drive-through and pay for the individual behind you. Your consideration will fill their heart with joy,

and they might try and begin a chain that shows proactive kindness!
Prepared products or blossoms can thoroughly light up somebody's day! Drop off a little treat with your new neighbors or your morning transport driver.

Give blood
A solitary blood gift can save the existence of 3 individuals. It's astounding — go into your neighborhood blood drive to give some blood, appreciate juice and treats, and leave realizing that you just did some serious great. On the off chance that you're feeling roused, visit the American Red Cross to get familiar with how you can have a blood drive event.[4]
Ordinarily, you must be north of 110 pounds (49.9 kg), something like 17 years old, and healthy to give.

By and large, you'll need to stand by 56
in the middle of between each blood gift.

Volunteer locally.
Good causes need energetic workers to
assist with accomplishing their
objectives. That could be you! Consider
an issue that you're enthusiastic about or
a need that you find in your nearby local
area. Then, at that point, look for the
good cause that means to help (on the
off chance that you don't know where to
look, begin on the web!). Giving your
time doesn't simply cause you to feel
astonishing, but on the other hand, it's an
extraordinary method for giving back.[5]
Care about the climate? Jump into an
end-of-week ocean-side clean.
Perhaps you're energetic about little
dogs. Connect with your neighborhood's
altruistic culture and check whether they
need some additional assistance.

You could reside in a city where numerous vagrants are battling. Destitute asylums are continuously searching for compassionate, assistance.

Give cash to a cause you regard. Giving your investment funds to a noble purpose is an incredibly liberal demonstration. Give whatever might be possible to associations that you appreciate. Your gift will permit lots of energetic, learned individuals to accomplish something beneficial on the planet and address significant issues confronting individuals today. Recollect that even a little can have a major effect. Lastly, vet the causes you're giving to [6] Research your decision of noble cause first (there are tricksters out there hoping to take liberal people groups' cash!) Pay special attention to copies — a few associations will attempt to trick you by picking comparative names to notable organizations

Assuming you're uncertain, ask the foundation for composing materials on their projects and funds

Utilize your abilities and skill to help. Your experience and information are important resources. In this way, if you can share them with others — function as a coach, assist somebody with planning for a task in your field, or volunteer to educate. With your range of abilities, you might be in a novel situation to be an immense assistance to important organizations.[7]

Perhaps you played a game in school — like soccer. You can elect to mentor a group of youthful players hoping to get to the next level!

Is it true that you are a genius with numbers? Address the schools in your space and inquire as to whether they need any additional worker guides.

On the off chance that you made it far in an extreme profession, you can assist with tutoring somebody by simply getting everything rolling. Perhaps your companion of companion needs to break into tech — mentor them through the cycle!

You might chip in with wikiHow. Compose an article or alter existing articles to assist us with showing anybody how to do anything (for nothing!).

Acclaim a bistro, craftsman, or business via online entertainment.

Positive posts are free, simple, and can be an immense assistance to new organizations. All around your town, individuals are in the middle of attempting to make their fantasies work out. A little permeability can mean everything — so on the off chance that you experience somebody's work and believe it's perfect, be clear about it. Take to online entertainment and compose a rave survey. Not exclusively will you fill somebody's heart with joy — you could assist them with taking off![8]

Perhaps you saw a little, neighborhood craftsman perform; take to Twitter! "I just saw The Rotaries in San Jose. So great. Everybody requirements to look at them quickly!"

If you just ate another café that wowed you, share their Facebook page: "Just attempted Jeff's Grille and it was beyond words! Stop in before they're reserved!"

Monitor somebody who could require help.

Show sympathy to somebody battling, and you could have an enormous effect. Psychological sickness or significant life-altering situations can negatively affect a companion's prosperity. Stand by listening to them, commend their triumphs, and keep on minding them — because this can bring greater security and association into their life. Pay special attention to signs that somebody may be battling, then make a move to help:[9] Assist them with finding top assets and experts who can help

Research advisors that they can think about seeing

When they have a "win," regardless of whether it's little, overemphasize it: "You at long last wiped out that storeroom? Amazing, well done! I realize that was worrying you.

Spread uplifting news.

Some of the time the world can feel somewhat dim — light up somebody's day with a good. There are generally extraordinary things occurring out there

— locally, on the planet, or even in your friend network. Give your very best to ensure individuals around you get to encounter a portion of those features. This can have a gigantic effect, and it's really simple to do!

Research uplifting news occurring in this present reality (Was a feline saved from a tree? Did a researcher find another animal category?) and offer it openly in each discussion.
On the off chance that somebody you know finds an extraordinary line of work or an honor,

Chapter 4

Advantages of generosity

Helping other people could help you, as well.

From early on, we're informed that it's smarter to give than to get. Even though you might think this is only a platitude, it just so happens, there's a ton of truth behind that feeling.

At the point when we concentrated on how being liberal influences your life, we found that individuals with elevated degrees of generosity receive a wide range of rewards. Here are the advantages of generosity that stand apart the most.

More noteworthy fulfillment with life

Everybody needs to be content throughout everyday life, and generosity has all the earmarks of being a key fixing: 74% of high-generosity respondents detailed fulfillment with their lives, contrasted with 60% of low-generosity respondents. High-generosity respondents were likewise over two times as liable to report that they were "exceptionally fulfilled" with life.

This wasn't restricted to one part of life, it is possible that; it was in all cases. The high-generosity bunch was more joyful generally speaking in each perspective we got some information about, including fellowships, family, sentiment, and funds.

More companions
Generosity appears to assist with your public activity. The individuals who are

exceptionally liberal announced having more companions who might want to offer courtesies to them, for example,

Visiting them at the medical clinic
Assisting them with moving
Driving them to or from the air terminal
This gathering additionally had all the more dear companions. High-generosity respondents had a normal of 3.2 dear companions, while those in the low-generosity bunch had a normal of 2.6.

 More grounded associations with individuals they know
Having a bigger group of friends wasn't the main advantage of being liberal. Individuals high in generosity likewise will generally have further associations with others, considering to be 66% of them felt near individuals they know. Just half

of the individuals low in generosity felt something similar.

More joyful with their vocations

Taking into account how much time you spend at work, you need to feel content with your work. On the off chance that not, you're taking a gander at eight hours of the day of wanting to be elsewhere.

This is one of the areas where there was a huge gap between high-generosity and low-generosity individuals. Of those high in generosity, 70% communicated fulfillment with their positions. Of those low in generosity, just 49% had that equivalent fulfillment.

A more uplifting perspective

Your point of view has a tremendous effect on how blissful you are. Assuming you trust that what you're doing matters, you're likely going to partake in your life substantially more.

A full 81% of exceptionally liberal individuals accept life is significant - - that is 21% more than the people who are not liberal. Furthermore, a significant life might be the reason 77% of the more-liberal gathering said they feel blissful consistently, contrasted with 62% of the less selfless society.

Better physical and emotional wellness Considering that more liberal individuals are more joyful and more sure, you might have previously speculated that their psychological wellness is in better shape. High-generosity individuals were less inclined to feel a scope of pessimistic feelings, including sadness, discouragement, disregard, and uneasiness.

Here's one you might not have speculated - - there's likewise a relationship among's generosity and actual wellbeing. Those in the high-generosity bunch were bound to routinely eat a solid eating regimen and exercise.

Fulfillment with what you have Feeling some jealousy from time to time is typical. I question if anybody has carried on with existence while never needing something far off, like a more lavish vehicle or home.

While it's not unexpected to feel like this every so often, it's additionally essential to be content with what you have. That is almost certain assuming you're the liberal kind - - these respondents were happier with their homes, vehicles, and different belongings.

They were likewise less inclined to accept that having more cash would make them more joyful. All things considered, it doesn't give the idea that liberal individuals experience difficulty setting aside cash, even though a few types of generosity can include monetary gifts.

   Higher confidence
What you feel about yourself can mean for all aspects of your life for better or for more terrible, and there's proof that a liberal way of life is great for your confidence.

At the point when we inquired as to whether they were pleased with what their identity is, 74% of the great generosity bunch said OK. Among the low-generosity bunch, that dropped to 51%. Individuals with elevated degrees of generosity were likewise bound to say that they carried on with moral and upstanding lives.

An individual with high confidence (not self-image) might be all the more genuinely liberal where they offer yet don't expect something as a trade-off. They are only glad to give and see someone else blissful. They don't require something from you to cheer them up. Helping other people works on your confidence and feeling of direction. Individuals who volunteer their time, give a reason they care about, or help somebody needing help, have higher confidence and general prosperity.

You don't need to go to a haven or put yourself in peril during a catastrophic event to have an effect. Contemplate how great it feels when you share content internet based on something you're energetic about. Sharing is mindful and it is helping other people.

Require a moment to recognize how you to distinguish how you can have an effect. Who in your life might require some additional assistance? What causes do you feel called to assist with? Is there something locally, on the web, or in your space, that could utilize your gifts and time?

Make a rundown of your abilities, gifts, and things you are educated about, and contemplate how you can serve individuals with these characteristics that you have. Ponder these inquiries:

How long do I need to give?

What abilities do I have that a
not-for-profit, or that the local area, could
profit from?
Do I have assets to monetarily give?
Do I have things I don't need that could
end up being useful to another person?
What am I normally called to?
Do I like creatures, kids, and helping the
older?
By moving your reasoning towards
helping other people while doing
something important to you, your
confidence, feeling of direction, and
sensations of association increment
emphatically.
So evident! The part about helping other
people working on confidence/certainty

Generosity can be contingent or
unrestricted. It has to do with an
individual's intention and, it doesn't
matter, just like all friendly animals with

our plans and needs and wants in any case.

Generosity can completely change you Assuming that there's one important point from this, it's that being liberal can decisively affect your satisfaction. It can make you more joyful, and better, and work on your associations with others.

There is a wide range of ways of being liberal, from giving to a reason you have confidence into chipping in your time. Not exclusively will it benefit others, yet it could likewise help you